MAY 50 COLORING PAGES
FOR ADULTS RELAXATION

SHIH CHIEN HUA

PUBLISHED BY:
SHIH CHIEN HUA
Copyright © 2018

SEABIRD SHOP >50FOR

FB FAN PAGE

Disclaimer
The information contained in this book is for general information purposes only. The information is provided by the authors and while we endeavor to keep the information up to date and correct, we make no representations or warranties of any kind, express or implied, about the completeness, accuracy, reliability, suitability or availability with respect to the book or the information, products, services, or related graphics contained in the book for any purpose. Any reliance you place on such information is therefore strictly at your own risk.

MAY 1ST

note:

_____

_____

_____

MAY 2ND

note:

_____

_____

_____

MAY 3RD

note:

_____

_____

_____

MAY 4TH

note:

_____

_____

_____

MAY 5TH

note:

_____

_____

_____

MAY 6TH

note:

_____

_____

_____

MAY 7TH

note:

_____

_____

_____

MAY 8TH

note:

_____

_____

_____

MAY 9TH

note:

_____

_____

_____

MAY 10TH

note:

_____

_____

_____

MAY 11TH

note:

_____

_____

_____

MAY 12TH

note:

_____

_____

_____

MAY 13TH

note:

_____

_____

_____

MAY 14TH

note:

_____

_____

_____

MAY 15TH

note:

_____

_____

_____

MAY 16TH

note:

_____

_____

_____

MAY 17TH

note:

_____

_____

_____

MAY 18TH

note:

_____

_____

_____

MAY 19TH

note:

_____

_____

_____

MAY 20TH

note:

_____

_____

_____

MAY 21TH

note:

_____

_____

_____

MAY 22TH

note:

_____

_____

_____

MAY 23TH

note:

_____

_____

_____

MAY 24TH

note:

_____

_____

_____

MAY 25TH

note:

_____

_____

_____

MAY 26TH

note:

_____

_____

_____

MAY 27TH

note:

_____

_____

_____

MAY 28TH

note:

_____

_____

_____

MAY 29TH

note:

_____

_____

_____

MAY 30TH

note:

_____

_____

_____

MAY 31TH

note:

_____

_____

_____

MAY 32TH

note:

_____

_____

_____

MAY 33TH

note:

_____

_____

_____

MAY 34TH

note:

_____

_____

_____

MAY 35TH

note:

_____

_____

_____

MAY 36TH

note:

_____

_____

_____

MAY 37TH

note:

_____

_____

_____

MAY 38TH

note:

_____

_____

_____

MAY 39TH

note:

_____

_____

_____

MAY 40TH

note:

_____

_____

_____

MAY 41TH

note:

_____

_____

_____

MAY 42TH

note:

_____

_____

_____

MAY 43TH

note:

_____

_____

_____

MAY 44TH

note:

_____

_____

_____

MAY 45TH

note:

_____

_____

_____

MAY 46TH

note:

_____

_____

_____

MAY 47TH

note:

_____

_____

_____

MAY 48TH

note:

_____

_____

_____

MAY 49TH

note:

_____

_____

_____

MAY 50TH

note:

_____

_____

_____